THE WISDOM OF
JESUS

Compiled by Jean-Yves Leloup

Illustrations from *Les Très Riches Heures du Duc de Berry*

Abbeville Press   Publishers

New York   London   Paris

Cover illustration and vignettes by Danielle Siegelbaum

For the English-language edition
RESEARCH, TRANSLATION FROM THE FRENCH, AND BIBLIOGRAPHY:
John O'Toole
EDITOR: Jacqueline Decter
TYPOGRAPHIC DESIGN: Virginia Pope
PRODUCTION EDITOR: Owen Dugan

For the original edition
SERIES EDITORS: Marc de Smedt and Michel Piquemal
DESIGNER: Dominique Guillaumin/Cédric Ramadier

First edition
10 9 8 7 6 5 4 3 2 1

Library of Congress Cataloging-in Publication Data

Paroles de Jésus. English.
The wisdom of Jesus/compiled by Jean-Yves Leloup.
p. cm.
Includes bibliographical references.
ISBN 0-7892-0239-5
1. Jesus Christ—Teachings. I. Leloup, Jean-Yves. II. Title.
BS2415.A2P37 1996
226'.052—dc20
                                                        96–8010

To understand Jesus, we would have had to walk with him, step lightly down to the lake. To understand him, we would have had to return to Tiberias, catch our fish for the day there, grill it between two stones, and suddenly feel a hand laid upon our shoulder; after the tiring journey, this was the sign to take a seat.

Then to listen. Not to be surprised if Nature herself grew still—only those who think of themselves as wise feel unconcerned.

His voice is not as deep as one might think. It bears a trace of his smile, which in no way detracts from the profundity of what is said. His followers didn't understand immediately, yet it is enough to have felt the ocean spray lash one's face to know one must learn how to swim.

His words are like sown seeds, grain tossed into the earth that must survive the winter of our doubts and useless explanations. Then one day, "the Word is made flesh." That is, you understand because you have lived and put into practice what has been said. As if knowledge of love only revealed itself in acts—precise, tender, or proud acts that have a certain indescribable "gratuity" about them. Then we understand that Jesus's God is in us. Our limits are in fact infinite birthplaces. His teaching exists for us to make the very best of ourselves—and even something more. That pleasure doesn't keep shop along some street; it can be neither bought nor sold. Strange peace and joy, pure echoes of an unknown presence.

Jesus's words must not be separated from his life (for once we have someone who says what he thinks, and does what he says!). Let us then place each of his teachings once again in their context of shared wine and bread, of wounds and shed blood. For these words have a face and this face has all the faces of man. It is the face of the sage who teaches the way of bliss and patience when confronted with failure and suffering; the face of the man who walks the earth together with his hunger, his thirst, and his friends. He cares for the sick, he listens even more tenderly than he speaks, while the possessed find sparks of freedom in his gaze. He puts no label on certain kinds of behavior deemed unacceptable: whether one is an adulterer, a sinner, a criminal, or a prostitute, he sees only suffering men and women in search of an impossible love, in need of pardon or recognition.

"No one has ever spoken like this man," said the centurion, and his power to captivate, despite the caricatures that some have tried to paint throughout the centuries, has come down to us intact, continuing to inspire the maddest and the wisest of our fellow beings.

His words remain to be discovered now and forever, for the Gospel will be understood only by those who incarnate and live it. The Greek term *metanoia* invites us constantly to go beyond the mental, in other words, beyond the known. Although in general the term is wrongly translated as "conversion" or "penitence," it is rather an invitation to go beyond human intelligence that is closed upon itself. In its place we would have to write "metamorphosis" or "transformation" in our Gospel to understand its message better.

Dostoevsky knew nothing more beautiful than Christ; he perceived in Him what is both the most human and the most divine, the most enlightened and the most obscure. Beyond all the dualisms endlessly opposing death and life, crucifixion and resurrection, blood and light, he saw no other face that could bring together all faces in this way.

Jean-Yves Leloup

Suffer little children, and forbid them not, to come unto me, for of such is the kingdom of heaven.

Matthew 19:14

The Fall of the Rebellious Angels (detail)

Ask, and it shall be given you;

seek, and ye shall find;

knock, and it shall be opened unto you.

Matthew 7:7

David Praying

Ye are the salt of the earth, but if the salt have lost his savor, wherewith shall it be salted? It is thenceforth good for nothing, but to be cast out, and to be trodden under foot of men.

Matthew 5:13

March, Tilled Land (detail)

Which of you by taking thought

can add one cubit unto his stature?

Matthew 6:27

Before the Gates of Hell

Take therefore no thought for the morrow:

for the morrow shall take thought

for the things of itself.

Sufficient unto the day is the evil thereof.

Matthew 6:34

Lay not up for yourselves treasures upon earth,
where moth and rust doth corrupt, and where
thieves break through and steal.

But lay up for yourselves treasures in heaven, where
neither moth nor rust doth corrupt, and where thieves
do not break through nor steal.

For where your treasure is, there will your heart be also.

Matthew 6:19–21

Job (detail)

Judge not, that ye be not judged.

For with what judgment ye judge, ye shall be judged; and with what measure ye mete, it shall be measured to you again.

And why beholdest thou the mote that is in thy brother's eye, but considerest not the beam that is in thine own eye?

Or how wilt thou say to thy brother, "Let me pull out the mote out of thine eye"; and behold, a beam is in thine own eye?

Thou hypocrite, first cast out the beam out of thine own eye; and then shalt thou see clearly to cast out the mote out of thy brother's eye.

Matthew 7:1–5

The Apostles Setting out to Preach the Gospel (detail)

A new commandment I give unto you,

that ye love one another;

as I have loved you,

that ye also love one another.

By this shall all men know

that ye are my disciples,

if ye have love one to another.

John 13:34–35

The Invention of the Holy Cross (detail)

Ye have heard that it hath been said, "Thou shalt love thy neighbor, and hate thine enemy."

But I say unto you, love your enemies, bless them that curse you, do good to them that hate you, and pray for them which despitefully use you, and persecute you,

That ye may be the children of your Father which is in heaven: for he maketh his sun to rise on the evil and on the good, and sendeth rain on the just and on the unjust.

For if ye love them, which love you, what reward have ye? Do not even the publicans the same?

And if ye salute your brethren only, what do ye more than others? Do not even the publicans so?

Be ye therefore perfect, even as your Father which is in heaven is perfect.

Matthew 5:43–48

The Fall of the Rebellious Angels (detail)

Then came Peter to him, and said, "Lord, how oft shall my brother sin against me, and I forgive him? Till seven times?"

Jesus saith unto him, "I say not unto thee until seven times, but until seventy times seven."

Matthew 18:21–22

Christ and the Woman of Canaan (detail)

Blessed are the poor in spirit:

    for theirs is the kingdom of heaven.

Blessed are they that mourn:

    for they shall be comforted.

Blessed are the meek:

    for they shall inherit the earth.

Blessed are they which do hunger and thirst

    after righteousness: for they shall be filled.

Blessed are the merciful:

    for they shall obtain mercy.

Blessed are the pure in heart:

    for they shall see God.

Blessed are the peacemakers:

    for they shall be called the children of God.

Matthew 5:3–9

February (detail)

Unto what is the kingdom of God like? And whereunto shall I resemble it?

It is like a grain of mustard seed, which a man took, and cast into his garden: and it grew, and waxed a great tree; and the fowls of the air lodged in the branches of it.

Luke 13:18–19

View of a Battle (detail)

Then there arose a reasoning among them, which of them should be greatest.

And Jesus, perceiving the thought of their heart, took a child, and set him by him,

And said unto them, "Whosoever shall receive this child in my name receiveth me, and whosoever shall receive me receiveth him that sent me. For he that is least among you all, the same shall be great."

Luke 9:46–48

Purgatory (detail)

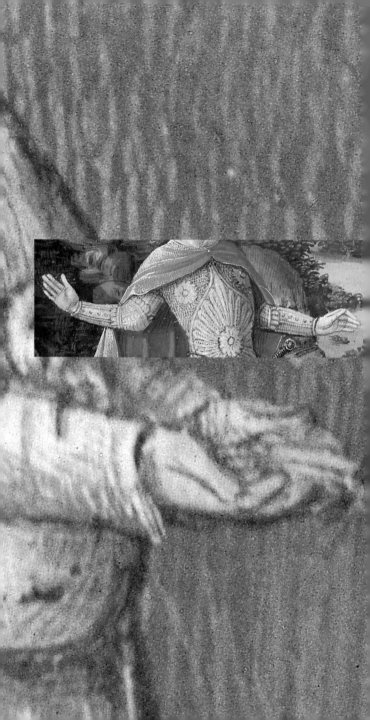

Therefore when thou doest thine alms, do not sound a trumpet before thee, as the hypocrites do in the synagogues and in the streets, that they may have glory of men. Verily I say unto you, they have their reward.

But when thou doest alms, let not thy left hand know what thy right hand doeth,

That thine alms may be in secret.

Matthew 6:2–4

David Praying (detail)

Behold, a sower went forth to sow; and when he sowed, some seeds fell by the way side, and the fowls came and devoured them up.

Some fell upon stony places, where they had not much earth; and forthwith they sprung up, because they had no deepness of earth;

And when the sun was up, they were scorched; and because they had no root, they withered away.

And some fell among thorns; and the thorns sprung up, and choked them.

But other fell into good ground, and brought forth fruit, some an hundredfold, some sixtyfold, some thirtyfold.

Who hath ears to hear, let him hear.

Matthew 13:3–9

October, Sowing (detail)

And when thou prayest, thou shalt not be as the hypocrites are, for they love to pray standing in the synagogues and in the corners of the streets, that they may be seen of men. Verily I say unto you, they have their reward.

But thou, when thou prayest, enter into thy closet, and when thou hast shut thy door, pray to thy Father which is in secret; and thy Father which seeth in secret shall reward thee openly.

Matthew 6:5–6

Celebration of the Mass in the Sainte-Chapelle (detail)

Verily, verily, I say unto thee, Except a man be born of water and of the Spirit, he cannot enter into the kingdom of God.

That which is born of the flesh is flesh; and that which is born of the Spirit is spirit.

John 3:5–6

Purgatory (detail)

The wind bloweth where it listeth,

and thou hearest the sound thereof,

but canst not tell whence it cometh,

and whither it goeth:

so is every one that is born of the Spirit.

John 3:8

Rest during the Flight into Egypt (detail)

Enter ye in at the strait gate. For wide is the gate, and broad is the way, that leadeth to destruction, and many there be which go in thereat.

Because strait is the gate, and narrow is the way, which leadeth unto life, and few there be that find it.

Matthew 7:13–14

Purgatory (detail)

I will have mercy, and not sacrifice.

Matthew 9:13

Christ Is Led to the Hall of Judgment (detail)

For there is nothing covered,

that shall not be revealed;

and hid,

that shall not be known.

Matthew 10:26

The Visitation (detail)

Les Très Riches Heures du Duc de Berry

The illustrations in this book are taken from the fifteenth-century masterpiece of miniature illumination *Les Très Riches Heures du Duc de Berry*.

A Book of Hours was a breviary for laymen of nobility who wanted a complete calendar of daily prayers embellished with beautifully detailed illuminations. The iconography teaches us about faith in general, as well as about the day-to-day life of that bygone era.

For all the reproductions in this work: © Giraudon.

With the permission of the Musée Condé de Chantilly and Faksimilé Verlag.

The Gospel texts reproduced here are from the admirable King James Version of the Bible, a high point of English prose first published in 1611. Because of its eloquence, thoroughly natural idiom, and elevated style, this translation continues to be the preferred Bible for many readers of English.

November

Selected Bibliography

Studies of the historical and spiritual figure of Jesus and his legacy abound. Here are a few suggestions:

Barclay, William. *The Mind of Jesus*. New York: HarperCollins, 1976 (paperback).

———. *Jesus as They Saw Him: New Testament Interpretations of Jesus*. Grand Rapids, Mich.: William B. Eerdman's, 1994 (reprint).

Crossan, J. D. *Jesus: A Revolutionary Biography*. San Francisco: HarperSan Francisco, 1995.

———. *The Historical Jesus: The Life of a Mediterranean Jewish Peasant*. San Francisco: HarperSan Francisco, 1992. (A much more in-depth study by the same author.)

Grant, Michael. *Jesus: An Historian's Review of the Gospels*. New York: Collier, 1992 (first published 1977).

Mitchell, Stephen. *The Gospel According to Jesus: A New Translation and Guide to His Essential Teachings for Believers and Unbelievers*. New York: Harper-Perennial, 1991.

Some general approaches to the New Testament:

Ackroyd, P. R., and C. F. Evans, eds. *The Cambridge History of the Bible: From the Beginnings to Saint Jerome*. Cambridge: Cambridge University Press, 1992 (first printed 1970).

Barrett, C. K., ed. *The New Testament Background: Writings From Ancient Greece and the Roman Empire that Illuminate Christian Origins*. San Francisco: HarperSan Francisco, 1988 (revised edition).

Kee, Howard Clark. *Understanding the New Testament*. Englewood, N.J.: Prentice Hall, 1993 (fifth edition). (An illustrated survey of the literary origins of the New Testament.)